WG

The Book of
Football Wisdom

The Book of
Football Wisdom

Common Sense and Uncommon Genius
From 101 Gridiron Greats

Compiled and Edited by Criswell Freeman

WALNUT GROVE PRESS
Nashville, TN
(615) 256-8584

ISBN 1-887655-18-2

The ideas expressed in this book are not, in all cases, exact quotations, as some have been edited for clarity and brevity. In all cases, the author has attempted to maintain the speaker's original intent. In some cases, material for this book was obtained from secondary sources, primarily print media. While every effort was made to ensure the accuracy of these sources, the accuracy cannot be guaranteed. For additions, deletions, corrections or clarifications in future editions of this text, please write WALNUT GROVE PRESS.

Printed in the United States of America
Cover Design by Mary Mazer
Typesetting & Page Layout by Sue Gerdes
Edited by Alan Ross and Angela Beasley
2 3 4 5 6 7 8 9 10 •   98 99 00 01

ACKNOWLEDGMENTS
The author gratefully acknowledges the helpful support of Angela Beasley, Dick and Mary Freeman, and Mary Susan Freeman. Special appreciation is extended to Alan Ross for his tireless research and thoughtful advice.

Dedicated to Christopher Raquet

Our Family's Latest Athletic Hero

Table of Contents

Introduction 13

Chapter 1: Hard Work 15

Chapter 2: Toughness 23

Chapter 3: All-Purpose Advice........................ 33

Chapter 4: Success 43

Chapter 5: Leadership 55

Chapter 6: Life... 61

Chapter 7: Sportsmanship and Teamwork .. 69

Chapter 8: Preparation 77

Chapter 9: Adversity 83

Chapter 10: Coaching...................................... 91

Chapter 11: Attitude.. 103

Chapter 12: Winning and Losing 115

Chapter 13: Strategy 127

Chapter 14: The Great Ones........................... 135

Chapter 15: Observations 143

Sources 155

Introduction

Art imitates life, and football imitates war. In football, as in battle, victory depends upon sufficient training, careful planning, adequate resources, superior manpower and proper motivation. At the line of scrimmage, foot soldiers engage in hand-to-hand combat. Behind center, a commanding officer takes the snap. From the sidelines, a general and his staff devise strategy and inspire the troops. In the press box, owners and administrators provide civilian oversight. And the whole spectacle is carefully watched by millions of excited partisans.

Thankfully, football is a battle without permanent casualties. With few exceptions, player injuries are fleeting and soon forgotten. But lessons learned on the field of play may last a lifetime.

This book details the insights and humor of the gridiron's greatest warriors. Their collective wisdom sheds illumination on the game of football and the game of life.

In his memoirs, William Tecumseh Sherman wrote, "War is cruelty, and you cannot refine it." But before his death in 1891, Sherman witnessed the birth of a refined form of combat: American football. At the Battle of Fredericksburg, Sherman's nemesis, Robert E. Lee, observed, "It is well that war is so terrible, lest we should grow too fond of it." Americans still hate the tragedy of war, but we've come to love dearly the warrior sport that imitates it.

1

Hard Work

America has George Washington and football has Walter Camp. Washington will forever be "The Father of His Country," and Camp is the indisputable father of American football.

As a student at Yale, Camp proposed rule changes that transformed English-style rugby into the modern game of football. His innovations included the line of scrimmage, first downs, and a standardized scoring system.

Camp became Yale's first official football coach in 1893. His record was a not-too-shabby 218-11-8. In his spare time, Coach Camp promoted the game through articles and books.

Walter Camp was more than a coach, and he was more than a journalist. He was also a philosopher who had firm opinions about the dignity and utility of work. He claimed, "There is no substitute for hard work and effort beyond the call of duty. That is what strengthens the soul and ennobles one's character."

The following gems of wisdom concern hard work. As in the days of Walter Camp, there's still no substitute.

Hard Work

If you're going to be a champion,
you must be willing to pay a greater price
than your opponent.

Bud Wilkinson

You can be anything you want –
if you're willing to pay the price.

Eddie Robinson

Football is a form of life in which you have
to work if you're going to accomplish anything.

Cookie Gilchrist

The best thing I've learned in life is
that things have to be worked for. There's no
magic in making a winning team,
but there's plenty of work.

Knute Rockne

The key to my success?
Understanding that
there's no free lunch.

Lou Holtz

Hard Work

Man's finest hour is the moment
when he has worked his heart out
in a good cause and lies exhausted
on the field of battle – victorious.

Vince Lombardi

The price for victory is hard work.

Knute Rockne

Nobody who ever gave his best regretted it.

George Halas

A winner never quits
and a quitter never wins.

Knute Rockne

I have no magic formula. The only way I know
to win is through hard work.

Don Shula

Without self-discipline,
success is impossible. Period.

Lou Holtz

Good things happen to those who hustle.

Chuck Noll

We compete, not so much against
an opponent, but against ourselves.
The real test is this: Did I make
my best effort on every play?

Bud Wilkinson

If you don't give that extra effort
and make the sacrifices, if you don't work
hard at it, you won't make it because
the competition is too great.

Otto Graham

The harder you work,
the harder it is to surrender.

Vince Lombardi

I don't believe in miracles.
I believe in character.

Pat Dye

If you want to get better, work a little harder.

Jerry Rice

God doesn't want your ability – He wants your availability.

Bobby Bowden

The enjoyment of playing well supersedes the drudgery.

John Brodie

There are no office hours for champions.

Paul Dietzel

Nothing is work unless you'd rather be doing something else.

George Halas

2

Toughness

Football is a game played by warriors. To succeed, one must combine physical aggression with mental toughness. Anything less invites the game's twin Harpies: injury and defeat.

The legendary Red Blaik advised his players to "replace the spirit of good fellowship, which is antithetical to successful football, with the Spartanism that is indispensable."

History's greatest coaches and players were Spartan in their approach to the game. Lombardi was a ferocious competitor. So was Rockne. Bear Bryant was so tough that he once played a game with a broken leg. When asked about the pain, young Bryant replied, "It was only a little bone."

The following insights come from men who learned that the foundation of winning football isn't talent, and it isn't strategy. It's toughness.

Football is not a contact sport.
Football is a collision sport.
Dancing is a contact sport.
Duffy Daugherty

There is something in good men
that really yearns for discipline and
the harsh reality of head-to-head combat.
Vince Lombardi

Football, in its purest form,
remains a physical fight. As in any fight, if you
don't want to fight, it's impossible to win.
Bud Wilkinson

Guts win more games
than ability.

Bob Zuppke

The moderns claim it is exhausting
for a boy to play 60 minutes. Bunk!
Pudge Heffelfinger

The game has changed.
The ball is smaller, and the equipment is better.
But the players are just as tough.
Ernie Nevers

The great teams intimidate.
Not physically – psychologically.
Jim Finks

Why is football my kind of game?
Because it tells you something about
the character and intensity
of the people who play it.
Dick Vermeil

When you find your opponent's weak spot,
hammer it.

John Heisman

Hit the ball carrier
harder than he hits you.

Ray Nitschke

If a fellow makes a good hit on me,
I'll pat him on the rear and say "nice tackle."
But I'll be back.

Gayle Sayers

Hitting is the one thing that wins games.
You make mistakes, but if you're hitting,
things will eventually go your way.

John Mackey

Toughness

I wouldn't ever set out to hurt
      anybody deliberately unless it was,
         you know, important – like in
      a league game or something.

Dick Butkus

I can say with a clear conscience that I have
never knowingly bit another football player.
For one thing, I believe in good hygiene.

Conrad Dobler

My dad was in a circus act when I was a kid.
      He got shot out of a cannon.
      I'm an offensive lineman in the NFL.
      Sometimes I figure it would have been
      safer to go into the family business.

Bob Kuechenberg

I'm a kicker, but I'm tough.
      On kickoffs, I barrel through there and knock
      those runners right on my fanny.

Errol Mann

Everyone has some fear.
A man who has
no fear belongs in a
mental institution.
Or on special teams.

Walt Michaels

Football is brutal.
    But if you're nothing but a brute,
        you can't play it.

Bob Zuppke

Catching passes is mostly a matter
    of getting the jump on the other guy.
        When you get the jump,
            size doesn't matter.

Tommy McDonald

All the height, strength and speed
    in the world can be neutralized if the guy
    across from you gets a jump on the ball.

George Perles

Play with small hurts.

Vince Lombardi

My advice for defensive players:
Take the shortest route to the ball
and arrive in a bad humor.

Bowden Wyatt

The minute I think I'm getting mellow,
I'm retiring. Who ever heard
of a mellow winner?

Woody Hayes

In the end, the game comes down to one thing: man against man. May the best man win.

Sam Huff

3

All-Purpose Advice

On the gridiron, advice is never in short supply. Coaches implore players to "stay low," "keep your head up," "drive those legs," " square those shoulders," "pick up those knees," and "keep your mind on the game." Easier said than done.

The inimitable Ohio State coach, Woody Hayes, gave simple advice that applies both on and off the field. Hayes said, "Be a pragmatist. First, find out what works. Then keep doing it."

By building a football dynasty around a few simple principles, Woody applied his own pragmatic philosophy. First, he demanded toughness and total dedication from his players. Second, he demanded that they run the football. Again and again and again.

The following all-purpose advice comes courtesy of men who, like Hayes, discovered what worked. Now it's our turn.

Be polite,
treat everybody nice,
and take the world
as you find it.

Mother's Advice to the Selmon Brothers

Don't cuss. Don't argue with the officials.
And don't lose the game.

John Heisman

Do what's right. Do your best.
And treat other people like
they want to be treated.

Lou Holtz

Always spread out the credit,
and never point fingers.

Ken Anderson

Never get into an argument
about cesspools with an expert.

Grandmother's Advice to Grantland Rice

Never let yesterday take up
　　　too much of today.
Sign in Tex Schramm's Office

Forget the past – the future will give you
　　　plenty to worry about.
George Allen

If you're killing time, it's not murder.
　　　It's suicide.
Lou Holtz

The past is history.
Make the present good,
and the past will take
care of itself.

Knute Rockne

Build your empire on the firm foundation
of the fundamentals.

Lou Holtz

Learn from everyone, copy no one.

Don Shula

Try not to do too many things at once.
Know what you want, the number one
thing today and tomorrow.
Persevere and get it done.

George Allen

Once a day, do something
for somebody else.

Lou Holtz

Assert your dignity.

Jim Brown

Don't talk too much
or too soon.

Bear Bryant

If you want to catch more fish,
use more hooks.

George Allen

Don't burn your bridges
at both ends.

Bill Peterson

When in doubt, punt!

John Heisman

If you hate your job,
don't worry. You
won't have it long.

George Allen

There is no economy in buying cheap equipment. Buy only the best.

Knute Rockne

4

Success

Success is difficult to define, but we know it when we see it. In the 1950s, the name Oklahoma became synonymous with gridiron success under the thoughtful tutelage of Bud Wilkinson. In 17 years, the Sooners won three national titles, enjoyed four unbeaten seasons, and, during one remarkable streak, won 47 straight games.

Oklahoma's president, Dr. George L. Cross, was asked about his school's academic goals. He responded, "We're trying to build a university our football team can be proud of." High aspirations indeed.

Inches make a champion,
and the champion
makes his own luck.

Red Blaik

The spirit, the will to win and the will
to excel – these are the things that endure.
Vince Lombardi

You can achieve only that which you will do.
George Halas

The achiever is the only individual
who is truly alive. I see no difference in
a chair and the man who sits in the chair,
unless he's accomplishing something.
George Allen

I pray not for victory, but to do my best.
Amos Alonzo Stagg

Success is what you do with your ability.
It's how you use your talent.

George Allen

Success – it's what you do
with what you've got.

Woody Hayes

Success is about having,
and excellence is about being. Success is
about having money and fame. But
excellence is being the best you can be.

Mike Ditka

Success is living up to your potential.
That's all.

Joe Kapp

You get out of life, and out of football,
exactly what you put into it. When a person
realizes this and acts accordingly,
he is sure to succeed.

Bart Starr

Winning isn't getting ahead of others.
It's getting ahead of yourself.

Roger Staubach

In great attempts, it is glorious even to fail.

Vince Lombardi

,

Success

The thrill isn't in the winning,
it's in the doing.

Chuck Noll

Success is never final.
Failure is never fatal.

Joe Paterno

Winning is like shaving.
You do it every day, or you end up
looking like a bum.

Jack Kemp

Organization is a habit.

George Allen

My idea of success is to know that I could
play for anybody and have the respect around
the league of other players and coaches.
This, I think I accomplished.

Brian Piccolo

There's only one way to succeed in anything,
and that's give it everything. I do,
and I demand that my players do.

Vince Lombardi

Upon the field of friendly strife
are sown the seeds, that on other fields, on
other days, will bear the fruits of victory.

General Douglas MacArthur

Discover the talent that God has given you.
Then go out and make the most of it.

Steve Spurrier

I can't believe God put us
on this earth to be ordinary.

Lou Holtz

Each of us has been put on earth
with the ability to do something well.
We cheat ourselves and the world if
we don't use that ability as best we can.

George Allen

Morale and attitude
are the fundamental ingredients to success.
Bud Wilkinson

Success without honor is an unseasoned dish.
Joe Paterno

Being respected is more important
than being popular.
Lou Holtz

The quality of a person's life
is in direct proportion to his commitment
to excellence, regardless of his
chosen field of endeavor.
Vince Lombardi

Success isn't measured by money or power
or social rank. Success is measured
by your discipline and inner peace.

Mike Ditka

Happiness is being able to lay your head
on the pillow at night and sleep.

Herschel Walker

The only problem with doing
the impossible is that everybody expects you
to duplicate the impossible.

John McKay

The more successful you become,
the longer the yardstick people use
to measure you by.

Tom Landry

The minute you think you've got it made,
disaster is just around the corner.

Joe Paterno

Nobody becomes great without self-doubt.
But you can't let it consume you.

John McKay

There are a thousand reasons for failure
but not a single excuse.

Mike Reid

5

Leadership

The game of football has produced more than its share of celebrated leaders. Names like Rockne, Halas, Warner, Neyland and Bryant are firmly established in football lore. But the title of "greatest coaching legend of all time" may belong to Vince Lombardi. Lombardi captured championships, but he also captured the nation's imagination. Today, his inspirational words are a part of American folklore.

When asked about leadership, Lombardi responded, "Running a football team is no different than running any other organization — an army, a political party, a business. The principles are the same."

The leadership lessons that follow work equally well on or off the gridiron. Heed and lead.

Nobody wants to follow somebody
who doesn't know where he's going.

Joe Namath

Leadership is the ability to lift and inspire.

Paul Dietzel

Leadership, like coaching, is fighting
for the hearts and souls of men and
getting them to believe in you.

Eddie Robinson

Motivation is simple. You eliminate those who aren't motivated.

Lou Holtz

My coaching philosophy? Determine your
players' talents and give them every weapon
to get the most from those talents.

Don Shula

You win with people.

Woody Hayes

Lots of leaders want to be popular.
I never cared about that. I want to be respected.

Don Shula

A real executive goes around
with a worried look on his assistants.

Vince Lombardi

Organize. Deputize. And supervise.

Biff Jones

Good fellows are a dime a dozen,
but an aggressive leader is priceless.

Red Blaik

In the successful organization, no detail is
too small to escape close attention.

Lou Holtz

Apart from an innate grasp of tactical
concepts, a great coach must possess the
essential attributes of leadership which
mold men into a cohesive, fighting team
with an invincible will to victory.

General Douglas MacArthur

Leadership must be demonstrated, not announced.

Fran Tarkenton

6

Life

Every football coach has, at least once in his life, uttered the words "football is like life." Like most clichés, this one contains more than a sprinkling of truth.

Bob Zuppke, the colorful head coach at the University of Illinois, may have said it best. He observed, "The value of all art, whether in pigment or pigskin, lies to some degree in its resemblance to life."

The following words of wisdom come courtesy of pigskin artists who have left their marks on the gridiron canvas.

Yesterday is a
canceled check.
Today is cash on the line.
Tomorrow is a
promissory note.

Hank Stram

For a good life:
> Work like a dog. Eat like a horse.
> Think like a fox. And play like a rabbit.
>> *George Allen*

Live in a way that makes you feel good,
> and get your fun out of feeling good.
>> *Amos Alonzo Stagg*

If you're not in the parade,
> you watch the parade. That's life.
>> *Mike Ditka*

First become a winner in life.
Then it's easier to become a winner on the field.
Tom Landry

Football is like life.
It requires perseverance, self-denial,
hard work, sacrifice, dedication and
respect for authority.
Vince Lombardi

You can learn more character
on the two-yard line than anywhere else in life.
Paul Dietzel

Football, like life, is about change.

Hank Stram

In life, it's always fourth-and-one, and there
are those urging me to go for it.

Joe Gibbs

Every man is born with the ability
to do something well. This is what the Lord
intended him to do. Using that ability –
that's what life is all about.

George Allen

Football is a great deal like life.
It demands a man's personal commitment
toward excellence and toward victory,
even though he knows that ultimate
victory can never be completely won.

Vince Lombardi

My faith, my family, my city and my friends
are the valuable things in my life.

Art Rooney

Don't go to your grave with a life unused.

Bobby Bowden

The future is now.

George Allen

If you live long enough,
lots of nice things happen.

George Halas

There are no shortcuts
in life – only those
we imagine.

Frank Leahy

Never let hope
elude you. That is
life's biggest fumble.

Bob Zuppke

7

Sportsmanship and Teamwork

Don Shula once noted, "The one-man team is a complete and total myth." While all team sports require a certain element of cooperation, football is totally dependent upon teamwork. Even the greatest players cannot carry a squad single-handedly.

On July 4, 1776, Ben Franklin signed the Declaration of Independence, then turned to his fellow patriots and said, "We must all hang together, or assuredly we shall all hang separately."

Old Ben never coached a football game. But he delivered a great pre-game pep talk because he understood the same principle that Shula rediscovered two centuries later. Whether it's war on the field or in the field, teamwork wins.

Football is an honest game. It's true to life.
It's a game about sharing.
Football is a team game. So is life.

Joe Namath

Football is not an "I" game.
It's a "we" game.

Pat Dye

Success is based on what the team does,
not how you look.

Knute Rockne

The greatest accomplishments occur, not
when you do something for yourself, but
when you do something for other people.

Ronnie Lott

Team guts always beats
       individual greatness.

Bob Zuppke

One guy can't do it by himself, and it's
    a matter of recognizing this and giving
      others their share of the credit.

Archie Manning

You can accomplish anything as long as
    you don't care who gets the credit.

Blanton Collier

If a team is to reach its potential,
    each player must be willing to subordinate
    his personal goals to the good of the team.

Bud Wilkinson

The only true satisfaction a player receives
is the satisfaction that comes from being
part of a successful team, regardless
of his personal accomplishments.

Vince Lombardi

The essence of the game is not "fun,"
but the soul-satisfying awareness that comes
from communal work and sacrifice.

Red Blaik

Play for your own self-respect
and the respect of your teammates.

Dan McGugin

Discipline, with team togetherness,
wins football games.

Johnny Vaught

Individual commitment to a group effort –
that is what makes a team work, a company
work, a society work, a civilization work.

Vince Lombardi

The first thing any coaching staff must do
is weed out selfishness. No program
can be successful with players who
put themselves ahead of the team.

Johnny Majors

For when that One Great Scorer comes
to mark against your name,
He writes – not that you won or lost –
but how you played the game.

Grantland Rice

If the coach insists upon hard play
but clean play, the team will do likewise.
Knute Rockne

When it comes to celebrating,
act like you've been there before.
Terry Bowden

Be a gracious winner
and an understanding loser.
Joe Namath

There never was a champion who to himself
was a good loser. There's a vast difference
between a good sport and a good loser.
Red Blaik

One man practicing
sportsmanship is better
than a hundred
teaching it.

Knute Rockne

All that I accomplish is not because of me. It's because of God and the offensive line.

Walter Payton

8

Preparation

In football, as in Boy Scouts, the motto is, "Be prepared." On the gridiron, the thin line between winning and losing is often a matter of preparation. Green Bay Packers legend Don Hutson noted, "For every pass I ever caught in a game, I caught a thousand in practice." The great defensive end Charles Haley once observed, "If you sacrifice early, you'll win late."

The lesson of preparation is one that applies far beyond the sidelines. Here are some observations from men who learned one of life's most important lessons: It pays to be prepared. Scout's honor.

You play the way you practice.
Practice the right way, and
you'll play the right way.

Pop Warner

Practice doesn't make perfect.
Perfect practice makes perfect.

Johnny Majors

Always have a plan and believe in it.

Chuck Knox

In truth, I've never known a man
worth his salt who, deep down in his heart,
didn't appreciate discipline.

Vince Lombardi

Preparation is as necessary to successful
coaching as weather is to the weather man –
there must be some of it every day.

Bobby Dodd

First we will be best, then we will be first.

Lou Holtz

Preparation

You have to be willing to out-condition
your opponents.

Bear Bryant

You can't be fat and fast, too;
so lift, run, diet and work.

Hank Stram

To break training without permission
is an act of treason.

John Heisman

Did you know that the ball is actually
in play for only 12 minutes in a 60-minute
football game? Why should a football player
be leg weary after only 12 minutes of action?
It makes me laugh!

Pudge Heffelfinger

Spectacular achievements are always
preceded by unspectacular preparation.

Roger Staubach

Everybody is looking for instant success,
but it doesn't work that way. You build
a successful life one day at a time.

Lou Holtz

Luck is what happens when
preparation meets opportunity.

Darrell Royal

First, I prepare. Then I have faith.

Joe Namath

We spend more time in the classroom
than we do on the playing field.

Otto Graham

Winning is the science
of being totally prepared.

George Allen

You've got to be in a position for luck
to happen. Luck doesn't go around
looking for a stumblebum.

Darrell Royal

9

Adversity

Adversity is as much a part of football as kickoffs and touchdowns. Lou Holtz fought through his own tough times in 1980 when his Arkansas squad lost four straight games. After a 31-7 loss to SMU, Holtz spoke for losing coaches everywhere as he opened his television show with these words: "Welcome to the Lou Holtz Show. Unfortunately, I'm Lou Holtz."

Sometimes, adversity takes the form of inclement weather. On the last day of the year in 1967, Green Bay defeated the Cowboys in a championship game that came to be known as the "Ice Bowl." Played on frozen Lambeau Field, the game was a test of man against nature. In his pregame speech, Coach Lombardi warned his players, "To be a winner, you've got to be bigger than the weather."

Would you appreciate a sure-fire recipe for surviving adversity? Start with Lombardi's toughness. Mix in a generous helping of good-natured humor. Then add the quotations that follow.

Adversity

It's not whether you get knocked down,
it's whether you get up.

Vince Lombardi

I don't care how good a driver you are,
you may have a wreck.

Mike Garrett

You don't know a ladder has splinters
until you slide down it.

Bum Phillips

The road to Easy Street goes
through the sewer.

John Madden

It's a short trip from
the penthouse
to the outhouse.

Paul Dietzel

In losing, we learn a lot of football.

Bill Alexander

Difficulties in life are intended
to make us better, not bitter.

Dan Reeves

In a crisis, don't hide
behind anything or anybody.
They're going to find you anyway.

Bear Bryant

You never know how a horse will pull
until you hook him to a heavy load.

Bear Bryant

You don't develop good teeth
by eating mush.

Red Blaik

In life, you'll have your back up against
the wall many times. You might as well
get used to it.

Bear Bryant

I like to rehash the old days,
    but somehow I never replay games like
the one in 1916 when I was coaching SMU
    and Rice beat us 146-3.

Ray Morrison

The sun doesn't shine on the same dog
every day. But we sure as heck didn't expect
a near-total eclipse.

Steve Sloan

It's how you show up
at the showdown
that counts.

Homer Norton

Experience is not what
happens to a man.
It's what a man
does with what
happens to him.

Chuck Knox

10

Coaching

Coaches, like writers and politicians, must occasionally rely on hyperbole. Before a big game, Hall-of-Famer Tad Jones proclaimed, "Gentlemen, you are about to play football for Yale. Never again in your life will you do anything so important."

Football's most famous half-time sermon was delivered by Knute Rockne. Knute began by telling his players of a touching deathbed conversation with Notre Dame legend George Gipp. Then, in the hushed silence of the locker room, Rockne quoted Gipp: "Sometimes, when things are wrong and the breaks are beating the boys, tell them to win one for the Gipper." The Fighting Irish returned to the field and granted Gipp's request.

Not all of us are gifted with the persuasive powers of Tad Jones or Knute Rockne. Wake Forest coach Chuck Mills spoke for the rest of us when he lamented, "I give the same halftime speech over and over. It works best when my players are better than the other team's players."

If you find yourself coaching a team when things are going wrong and the breaks are beating the boys, consider advice on the following pages. And, if all else fails, get better players.

Bear Bryant's Three Rules for coaching:
1. Surround yourself with people
   who can't live without football.
2. Recognize winners.
   They come in all forms.
3. Have a plan for everything.

What makes a good coach?
            Complete dedication.

George Halas

The secret to winning
      is constant, consistent management.

Tom Landry

The successful coach
is the one who can sell
the Spartan approach.

Red Blaik

You must learn how to hold a team together.
You must lift some men up, calm others down,
until finally they've got one heartbeat.
Then you've got yourself a team.

Bear Bryant

Coaches have to watch for
what they don't want to see and
listen to what they don't want to hear.

John Madden

The most successful coaches on any level
teach the fundamentals.

John McKay

The worst mistake any coach can make
is not being himself.

Charlie McClendon

I never tell my players anything
I don't absolutely believe myself.

Vince Lombardi

Put your information across
slowly and repeat it over and over again!
Take a difficult point and make it so simple
that it will become clear even to the dullard.

Knute Rockne

A team should never practice on a field
that is not lined. Your players have to become
aware of the field's boundaries.

John Madden

Look for players with character and ability.
But remember, character comes first.

Joe Gibbs

A team in an ordinary frame of mind
will do ordinary things. A properly motivated
team will do extraordinary things.

Knute Rockne

Coaching isn't a great mystery.
It's just hard work, determination,
and inspiration at the right moment.

Bob Zuppke

You can motivate players
better with kind words
than you can with a whip.

Bud Wilkinson

No coach sure of himself and his team
    constantly bawls out the athletes.
Jock Sutherland

Never leave the field with a boy feeling
    you're mad at him. You can chew him out,
      but then pat him on the shoulder.
Jake Gaither

The fewer rules a coach has,
the fewer rules there are for players to break.
John Madden

A spoonful of humor
    makes the message go down easier.
Frank Leahy

It's bad coaching to blame your boys
for losing a game, even if it's true.

Jake Gaither

Either love your players
or get out of coaching.

Bobby Dodd

Coach a boy as if he were your own son.

Eddie Robinson

Sure, luck means a lot in football.
Not having a good quarterback is bad luck.
Don Shula

Some coaches pray for wisdom.
I pray for 260-pound tackles.
They'll give me plenty of wisdom.
Chuck Mills

You need material.
Any diamond cutter, with craftsmanship,
can trim the uneven stone and polish it to
brilliance. But I never heard of anyone
doing it with a hunk of coal.
Matty Bell

No matter how successful he is,
every coach eventually reaches a point where
a lot of people want somebody else.
Father's Advice to Bud Wilkinson

A coach is often responsible
to an irresponsible public.
Bob Zuppke

On this team, we're all united in a common goal: to keep my job.

Lou Holtz

11

Attitude

Only two men have been elected to the College Football Hall of Fame as both player and coach. The first was Amos Alonzo Stagg; the second was Bobby Dodd. Dodd was an All-American quarterback at Tennessee and a highly successful coach at Georgia Tech. He was also an amateur psychologist.

Coach Dodd believed in the self-fulfilling prophecy, so he wanted his boys thinking happy, positive thoughts. Dodd said, "If you think you're lucky, you're right."

The quotations that follow will help you maintain a positive approach to life. And if you think that thinking positive thoughts makes you lucky, you're right. Think about it.

Attitude

Morale is something
you don't put on like an overcoat.
You build on it, day by day.

Fielding Yost

The key to winning is poise under stress.

Paul Brown

If you're going to take gambles,
you must have one thing: self-confidence.

Don Shula

Believe deep down in your heart
that you're destined to do great things.

Joe Paterno

Attitude is not just
the way you think –
it's the way you live.

Fielding Yost

We don't care how big or strong
opponents are as long as they are human.

Bob Zuppke

It doesn't matter how big or tall or wide you are.
It has to do with your desire and ability.

Barry Sanders

Courage means being afraid to do something,
but still doing it.

Knute Rockne

You live up – or down – to your expectations.

Lou Holtz

Even if you aren't number one, you should
have the attitude that you are number one.

Joe Paterno

You can do anything you want to do.
You may have to do it a little differently,
but you can do it.

Father's Advice to Tom Dempsey

Confidence is contagious.
So is the lack of confidence.

Vince Lombardi

There are two kinds of discipline:
self-discipline and team discipline.
You need both.

Vince Dooley

Have a profound respect for discipline.

Shug Jordan

You have to play for yourself,
for your own pride and self-respect.

Dick Butkus

Nobody is going to wind you up
every morning and give you a pep talk.
So be a self-starter.

Lou Holtz

Only one thing is worse
than going into a game thinking you can't win.
That's going in convinced you can't lose.

Bernie Bierman

A team that won't be beat, can't be beat.

Johnny Poe

Being cold, like being determined to win,
is just a state of mind.

Woody Hayes

Fellows, you have 60 minutes for redemption
and a lifetime for regret.

Fritz Crisler

Many people flounder
about in life because they have no purpose.
Before it is possible to achieve anything,
an objective must be set.

George Halas

If you're bored with life –
if you don't get up every morning
with a burning desire to do things –
you don't have enough goals.

Lou Holtz

There's much more to playing quarterback than a strong arm, quick feet or great reflexes. Without the right approach to the game, talent means nothing.

Ken Anderson

The greatest quarterback is the guy who can make something happen. He isn't necessarily the guy who can throw the tightest spiral.

John Brodie

A quarterback's biggest problem –
and his most important job –
is gaining confidence.

Don Meredith

You may be scared to death,
but don't admit it, even to yourself.

Terry Bradshaw

Poise means never fighting yourself.

Bob Tyler

Confidence comes from hours and days
and weeks and years of constant work
and dedication.

Roger Staubach

A man is always better than he thinks.

Woody Hayes

I celebrate a victory when I start walking off
the field. By the time I get to the locker room,
I'm done.

Tom Osborne

If you aren't fired
with enthusiasm,
you'll be fired
with enthusiasm.

Vince Lombardi

Cultivate cheerfulness.

Knute Rockne

12

Winning and Losing

It was Red Sanders, not Vince Lombardi, who said, "Winning isn't everything, it's the only thing." While some might dispute Sanders' win-at-all-cost philosophy, others would whole-heartedly agree.

Russ Grimm of the Washington Redskins once admitted, "I'd run over my mother to win the Super Bowl." Upon hearing of Grimm's remark, opponent Matt Millen replied, "I'd run over Grimm's mother, too." We're still waiting to hear from Mrs. Grimm.

It's amazing how little difference there
is between a winning effort and a losing one.

Norm Snead

All quitters are good losers.

Bob Zuppke

You're never a loser until you quit trying.

Mike Ditka

Losing is easy. It's not enjoyable,
but it's easy.

Bud Wilkinson

Almost all games are lost by the losers,
not won by the winners.

Robert Neyland

Before you can win a game,
you must first not lose it.

Chuck Noll

Winning is not a sometime thing;
it's an all-the-time thing. You don't do things
right once in a while. You do them right
all of the time.

Vince Lombardi

Never go to bed a loser.

Sign in George Halas' Office

Winning isn't everything,
        but wanting to win is.

Vince Lombardi

Winning is living. Every time you win,
you're reborn. When you lose, you die a little.

George Allen

Without winners,
        there wouldn't be any civilization.

Woody Hayes

Close only counts
        in horseshoes and hand grenades.

Frank Howard

Some guys prayed they wouldn't get hurt.
Others prayed they would do a good job.
I prayed we would win.

Bobby Layne

Winning is a habit.
Unfortunately, so is losing.

Vince Lombardi

Winning is the epitome of honesty.

Woody Hayes

One thing I don't like about losing
is the winkers. They don't know what to say,
so they just wink.

Tom Cahill

Winning and Losing

The difference between a hero
and an also-ran is the guy who hangs on
for one last gasp.

Paul Dietzel

One big play can win a football game.
No one knows when the big play
is coming up, therefore every player
must go all out on every play.

Vince Lombardi

Character is determined in the second half.

Bernie Casey

Don't give up at halftime. Concentrate on
winning the second half.

Bear Bryant

How do you win?
By getting average players to play good
and good players to play great.
That's how you win.

Bum Phillips

What makes a championship team?
Leadership, dedication, and teamwork.

Matty Bell

I've been playing this game for 18 years
and I haven't yet figured a way to get into
the end zone when you're on your butt.

Fran Tarkenton

No coach, no matter how successful,
ever completely escapes
the pressure of winning.

John McKay

A life of frustration is inevitable
for any coach whose main enjoyment
is winning.

Chuck Noll

Winning is only half of it.
Having fun is the other half.

Bum Phillips

If your whole state of happiness comes
from winning Super Bowls, you're going
to be unhappy a lot of the time.

Troy Aikman

You can be a hard but good loser.
Any coach or team that cannot lose and treat
opponents with respect has no right to win.

Knute Rockne

There is nothing wrong with losing
unless you learn to like it.

Paul Brown

A tie is like kissing your sister.

Duffy Daugherty

They say a tie is like kissing your sister.
I guess it's still better than
kissing your brother.

Lou Holtz

When you win, nothing hurts.

Joe Namath

I never believed a boy was too small.
You can't have too many good players. Good
players win games, not big players.

Lynn "Pappy" Waldorf

Who's interested in a loser's alibi?
Nobody.

Art Rooney

The problem here at Yale
is to win just enough to keep the alumni
sullen instead of mutinous.

Herman Hickman

Always remember that
Goliath was a
40-point favorite over
Little David.

Shug Jordan

13

Strategy

Everyone, it seems, is an expert on football. Before Super Bowl VI, President Richard Nixon, believing he saw a weakness in the Dallas defense, picked up the phone and called Miami Dolphins' coach Don Shula. Shula described the call this way: "Mr. Nixon alerted me that the Cowboys are a real strong team, but he told me, 'I think you can hit Warfield on the down-and-out.'"

Upon hearing of the conversation, Ex-President and Texan Lyndon Johnson couldn't resist calling Tom Landry. Johnson confided, "My prayers and my presence will be with you, but I don't plan to send any plays."

Dallas won by three touchdowns.

Modern football?
I haven't seen a new play since high school.

Red Grange

You don't beat people with surprises,
but with execution.

John McKay

There are few secrets in football. So execute.

Hank Stram

Football is blocking and tackling.
Everything else is mythology.

Vince Lombardi

You win championships
with hard-hitting defense. If you don't win
that game you don't win *the* game.

Fred Akers

Professional football has become
an exercise in the creation of doubt and in the
old war tactic of arriving at a given point
first with the most.

Tex Maule

Football is nothing more than a series of
actions, mistakes, and miscalculations. Punt
and make your opposition make the mistakes.

Bob Neyland

Michigan's success is due to a policy
of letting the enemy take the risk of fumbling
inside his forty-yard line.

Fielding Yost

Football games aren't won – they're lost.

Fielding Yost

You draw Xs and Os on a blackboard,
and that's not so difficult. I can even do it with
my left hand.

John McKay

I want the big play. I don't want the little
play, the average play. I want the *big* play.
I'm not going to stay up all night trying
to figure out how to gain three yards.

Sid Gillman

The biggest mistake coaches make is saying
they're going to establish the run or establish
the pass. It's better to establish first downs.

Sam Rutigliano

Find out what the other team wants to do.
Then take it away from them.

George Halas

Three things can happen when you put
a ball in the air – and two of them are bad.
Duffy Daugherty

The forward pass
is a cowardly, immoral play.
Jock Sutherland

You cannot win if you cannot run.
Hank Stram

The secret of blocking
is getting the right angle.
Bo McMillin

One thing never changes:
The team that controls the line of scrimmage
wins the game.
Bud Wilkinson

Playing quarterback is this:
You read the defense and take what's there.

Johnny Unitas

A receiver should run with his head.

Bernie Casey

Football is more mental than physical,
no matter how it looks from the stands.

Ray Nitschke

Special teams are vital.
Something important happens
on every kicking play.

Marv Levy

I don't talk too much about my battle plan,
even after the game is over.
I save it for another occasion.

George Halas

My philosophy?
Simplicity plus variety.

Hank Stram

14

The Great Ones

Hank Stram observed, "The game changes, but the *real* players don't." The following quotations describe "real" players. Whether it's Thorpe or Grange or Brown or Payton, the great ones are indeed different.

The first superstar of the gridiron was Pudge Heffelfinger, an All-American lineman from Yale. After graduation in 1892, Pudge became the first paid football player when he earned $500 for a single game. In leading the Allegheny Athletic Association of Western Pennsylvania to victory, Heffelfinger scored the game's only touchdown. Grantland Rice wrote, "There will never be another Heffelfinger." Possibly so, but if Granny were alive today, he would be forced to admit that many others have followed in Pudge's oversized footsteps.

Vince Lombardi's Green Bay Packers
rolled over people like a herd of street thugs
at a switch blade sale.

Mark Ribowsky

George Halas was a great man, and every day
I appreciate him more and more.

George Allen

Don Shula is just like Vince Lombardi.
You pay the price, but you get what you pay for.

Marv Fleming

Paul Brown has done more for pro football
than any coach I know.

Otto Graham

Heisman was the only man to play
both Hamlet and Harvard.

Dick Schaap

I never had a conversation with Fielding Yost
because my parents taught me
never to interrupt.

Ring Lardner

I'd say college football began with Rockne.

Ara Parseghian

All football came from Stagg.

Knute Rockne

Bear Bryant could take his'n and beat your'n,
or he could take your'n and beat his'n.

Bum Phillips

When Jim Thorpe hit me, it felt like
a locomotive followed by a 10-ton truck
rambling over the remains.

Knute Rockne

Red Grange was three or four men
and a horse – all rolled into one.

Damon Runyon

Bronco Nagurski broke bones.

Buff Donelli

Looking back, Jim Brown was even better
than I thought he was, and I thought
he was the best.

Gino Marchetti

The only way to stop Jim Brown
was to get him a movie contract.

Spider Lockhart

I was a running back drafted by the Chicago
Bears in the same year as Gale Sayers.
Talk about being at the right place
at the wrong time!

Brian Piccolo

Franco Harris faked me out so bad one time
that I got a 15-yard penalty
for grabbing my own face mask.

D. D. Lewis

Walter Payton's the best back in football.
I wish I had better words to describe him.

Bud Grant

I wouldn't say Earl Campbell was in a class
by himself, but I can tell you one thing:
It sure don't take long to call the roll.

Bum Phillips

The Great Ones

Bobby Layne never lost a game in his life.
Time just ran out on him.

Doak Walker

Catching a ball thrown by Johnny Unitas
was easy. You just looked over your shoulder,
and the ball was hanging up there
like a peach on a tree.

Jimmy Orr

Dick Butkus was like Moby Dick
in a goldfish bowl.

Steve Sabol

I tackle everybody and then throw them away
one at a time until I come to the one
with the ball.

"Big Daddy" Lipscomb

Raymond Berry was the best pass catcher
alive. He could get free on a subway platform
and catch buttered corn.

Jack Mann

The big players have got to come out
and make the big plays in the big games.

Deion Sanders

If they retired the numbers of all greats
at Notre Dame, there wouldn't be
any numbers left.

Terry Hanratty

There ain't much to being a football player,
if you're a football player.

Pudge Heffelfinger

Deep inside, we're still the boys of autumn, that magic time of the year that once swept us onto America's fields.

Archie Manning

15

Observations on the National Championship, the Super Bowl, and other Necessities of Life

We conclude with assorted thoughts on assorted topics.

When you're playing
for the National Championship,
it's not a matter of life and death.
It's more important than that.

Duffy Daugherty

On game day, I'm as nervous
as a pig in a packing plant.

Darrell Royal

The Super Bowl is
The Great American Time-out.
Time Magazine

The Super Bowl is global theatre.
Brent Musburger

Have Super Bowl tickets.
Will trade for a reliable car or truck.
Classified Ad in *Miami Herald* Prior to Super Bowl XXIII.

Getting paid extra money to play in
the Super Bowl is kind of like putting
sugar on top of ice cream.
Willie Davis

Anybody can kick in practice,
but kicking in the big games is something else.
Good kickers are as scarce
as good quarterbacks.

Ray Nitschke

Playing cornerback is like being on an island.
People can see you, but they can't help you.

Eddie Lewis

There's no tougher way to make easy money
than pro football.

Norm Van Brocklin

I'm on a seafood diet.
I eat every food I see.

Winston Hill

I'll eat anything that won't eat me.

Herman Hickman

The Book of Football Wisdom

Our scholarships are based on need.
We never take a boy unless we need him.
Duffy Daugherty

I never graduated from Iowa.
I was only there for two terms:
Truman's and Eisenhower's.
Alex Karras

I could have been a Rhodes Scholar,
except for my grades.
Duffy Daugherty

We offer no scholarships for rowing.
Clemson will never subsidize a sport where
a man sits on his butt and goes backward.
Frank Howard

The test of a quarterback is
where his team finishes.

Paul Brown

I don't do many endorsements.
I'd rather get doused by Gatorade
than bust my butt selling it.

Bill Parcells

Egotism is the anesthetic
that dulls the pain of stupidity.

Frank Leahy

When all is said and done,
more is usually said than done.

Lou Holtz

If "ifs" and "buts" were candy and nuts,
wouldn't it be a Merry Christmas?

Don Meredith

Running a marathon is like
   playing a very rough football game
   with no hitting above the waist.

Alan Page

I realize that whether or not I catch the ball,
   I'm gonna get hit, so why not hang on?

Danny Abramowicz

What's the secret to running?
   Just show 'em a leg, then take it away.

Jim Thorpe

I'm not a mean player.
   You'll notice I never pick on a player
   who has a number above 30.

Mike Ditka

Pro football gave me a good perspective.
   When I entered the political arena, I had
   already been booed, cheered, cut, sold,
   traded, and hung in effigy.

Jack Kemp

My mother called me Cupcake.
My father called me Doughnut.
The family settled on Cookie.

Cookie Gilchrist

You can't pay back,
but you can pay forward.

Woody Hayes

Gentlemen, it is better
to have died as a small boy
than to fumble this football.

John Heisman

I played six positions in ten years and
did none of them justice. So I decided to quit
while I was still on the bottom.

Alex Hawkins

If they ever drop a nuclear bomb
on this country, the only things that
will survive are Astroturf and Don Shula.

Bubba Smith

It's good to have a lineman
you can look straight in the belly button.
Larry Csonka

Two kinds of ballplayers aren't worth a darn:
One that never does what he's told, and
one who does nothin' *except* what he's told.
Bum Phillips

Before our last game, an anonymous fan left
a fruitcake for the coaches. I wouldn't let
them eat it. When you're 2 and 8, you don't
mess around with unsigned fruitcakes.
Lee Corso

When they run you out of town,
make it look like you're leading the parade.
Bill Battle

Any time you give a man something
he doesn't earn, you cheapen him.
Our kids earn what they get,
and that includes respect.

Woody Hayes

Work hard, stay positive, and get up early.
It's the best part of the day.

George Allen

We all have more talent than we'll ever use.

Lou Holtz

Fundamentals are more important
than plays themselves.

Bernie Bierman

Football! First you've got competition.
And you've got action. That's why
it's the greatest game there is.

George Halas

I miss football so much –
heck, I even miss the interceptions.

Archie Manning

Football has not come
anywhere near its zenith.

George Halas

Winning is never final, so bring on next season.

Bill Parcells

Sources

Danny Abramowicz 149
Troy Aikman 122
Fred Akers 128
Bill Alexander 86
George Allen 36, 38, 40, 41, 45, 46, 48, 50, 63, 65, 66, 82, 118, 136, 152
Ken Anderson 35, 111
Bill Battle 151
Matty Bell 100, 121
Bernie Bierman 109, 152
Red Blaik 23, 44, 59, 72, 74, 87, 93
Bobby Bowden 21, 66
Terry Bowden 74
Terry Bradshaw 111
John Brodie 21, 111
Jim Brown 38
Paul Brown 104, 123, 148
Bear Bryant 23, 39, 80, 86, 87, 92, 94, 120
Dick Butkus 28, 108
Tom Cahill 119
Walter Camp 15
Bernie Casey 120, 132
Blanton Collier 71
Lee Corso 151
Fritz Crisler 109
George L. Cross 43

Larry Csonka 151
Duffy Daugherty 24, 124, 131, 144, 147
Willie Davis 145
Paul Dietzel 21, 56, 64, 85, 120
Mike Ditka 46, 52, 63, 116, 149
Conrad Dobler 28
Bobby Dodd 79, 99, 103
Buff Donelli 138
Vince Dooley 108
Pat Dye 20, 70
Jim Finks 26
Marv Fleming 136
Jake Gaither 98, 99
Mike Garrett 84
Joe Gibbs 65, 96
Cookie Gilchrist 16, 150
Sid Gillman 130
Otto Graham 20, 82, 136
Red Grange 128
Bud Grant 139
Russ Grimm 115
George Halas
    22, 45, 66, 92, 110, 130, 133, 153
Charles Haley 77
Terry Hanratty 141
Alex Hawkins 150

Woody Hayes 31, 33, 46, 58, 109, 112, 118, 119, 150, 152
Pudge Heffelfinger 26, 80, 141
John Heisman 27, 35, 40, 80, 150
Herman Hickman 125, 146
Winston Hill 146
Lou Holtz 17, 19, 35, 36, 38, 50, 51, 57, 59, 79, 81, 83, 102, 106, 108, 110, 124, 148, 152
Frank Howard 118, 147
Sam Huff 32
Don Hutson 77
Biff Jones 59
Tad Jones 91
Shug Jordan 108, 126
Joe Kapp 46
Alex Karras 147
Jack Kemp 48, 149
Chuck Knox 78, 90
Bob Kuechenberg 28
Tom Landry 53, 64, 92
Ring Lardner 137
Bobby Layne 119
Frank Leahy 67, 98, 148
Marv Levy 133
D. D. Lewis 139
Eddie Lewis 146

"Big Daddy" Lipscomb 140
Spider Lockhart 138
Vince Lombardi 18, 20, 24, 31, 45, 47, 49, 51, 55, 58, 64, 65, 72, 73, 79, 80, 83, 84, 95, 107, 113, 117, 118, 119, 120, 128, 129
Ronnie Lott 70
Douglas MacArthur 49, 59
John Mackey 27
John Madden 84, 94, 96, 98
Johnny Majors 73, 78
Errol Mann 28
Jack Mann 140
Archie Manning 71, 142, 153
Gino Marchetti 138
Tex Maule 129
Charlie McClendon 95
Tommy McDonald 30
Dan McGugin 72
John McKay 53, 54, 94, 121, 128, 130
Bo McMillin 131
Don Meredith 111, 148
Walt Michaels 29
Matt Millen 115
Chuck Mills 91, 100
Ray Morrison 88
Brent Musburger 145

Joe Namath 56, 70, 74, 81, 125
Ernie Nevers 26
Bob Neyland 117, 129
Ray Nitschke 27, 133, 146
Chuck Noll 19, 48, 117, 122
Homer Norton 89
Jimmy Orr 140
Tom Osborne 112
Alan Page 149
Bill Parcells 148, 154
Ara Parseghian 137
Joe Paterno 48, 51, 54, 104, 107
Walter Payton 76
George Perles 30
Bill Peterson 40
Bum Phillips 84, 121, 122, 137, 139, 151
Brian Piccolo 49, 139
Johnny Poe 109
Dan Reeves 86
Mike Reid 54
Mark Ribowsky 136
Grantland Rice 73, 135
Jerry Rice 20
Eddie Robinson 16, 56, 99
Knute Rockne 16, 18, 37, 42, 70, 74, 75, 91, 95,
    96, 106, 114, 123, 137, 138

Art Rooney 66, 125
Darrell Royal 81, 82, 144
Damon Runyon 138
Sam Rutigliano 130
Steve Sabol 140
Barry Sanders 106
Deion Sanders 141
Red Sanders 115
Gayle Sayers 27
Dick Schaap 137
Don Shula 19, 38, 58, 69, 100, 104, 127
Steve Sloan 88
Bubba Smith 150
Norm Snead 116
Steve Spurrier 50
Amos Alonzo Stagg 45, 63
Bart Starr 47
Roger Staubach 47, 81, 112
Hank Stram 62, 65, 80, 128, 131, 134, 135
Jock Sutherland 98, 131
Fran Tarkenton 60, 121
Jim Thorpe 149
Bob Tyler 111
Johnny Unitas 132
Norm Van Brocklin 146
Johnny Vaught 72

Sources

Dick Vermeil 26
Lynn "Pappy" Waldorf 125
Doak Walker 140
Herschel Walker 52
Pop Warner 78
Bud Wilkinson 16, 19, 24, 51, 71, 97, 116, 131
Bowden Wyatt 31
Fielding Yost 104, 105, 129
Bob Zuppke 25, 30, 61, 68, 71, 96, 101, 106, 116

WG

About the Author

Criswell Freeman is a Doctor of Clinical Psychology living in Nashville, Tennessee. He is the author of *When Life Throws You a Curveball, Hit It* and *The Wisdom Series* from WALNUT GROVE PRESS. He is also a published country music songwriter.

About Wisdom Books

Wisdom Books chronicle memorable quotations in an easy-to-read style. Written by Criswell Freeman, this series provides inspiring, thoughtful and humorous messages from entertainers, athletes, scientists, politicians, clerics, writers and renegades. Each title focuses on a particular region or special interest.

Combining his passion for quotations with extensive training in psychology, Dr. Freeman revisits timeless themes such as perseverance, courage, love, forgiveness and faith.

"Quotations help us remember the simple yet profound truths that give life perspective and meaning," notes Freeman. "When it comes to life's most important lessons, we can all use gentle reminders."

The Wisdom Series
by Dr. Criswell Freeman

Wisdom Made In America
ISBN 1-887655-07-7

The Book of Southern Wisdom
ISBN 0-9640955-3-X

The Wisdom of the Midwest
ISBN 1-887655-17-4

The Book of Texas Wisdom
ISBN 0-9640955-8-0

The Book of Florida Wisdom
ISBN 0-9640955-9-9

The Book of California Wisdom
ISBN 1-887655-14-X

The Book of New England Wisdom
ISBN 1-887655-15-8

The Book of New York Wisdom
ISBN 1-887655-16-6

The Book of Country Music Wisdom
ISBN 0-9640955-1-3

The Wisdom of Old-Time Television
ISBN 1-887655-64-6

The Golfer's Book of Wisdom
ISBN 0-9640955-6-4

The Wisdom of Southern Football
ISBN 0-9640955-7-2

The Book of Stock Car Wisdom
ISBN 1-887655-12-3

The Wisdom of Old-Time Baseball
ISBN 1-887655-13-1

The Book of Football Wisdom
ISBN 1-887655-18-2

Wisdom Books are available through booksellers everywhere.
For information about a retailer near you, call 1-800-256-8584.